Key Was Turned

WOMEN AT THE FOUNDING OF THE RELIEF SOCIETY

BARBARA B SMITH AND
SHIRLEY K. THOMAS

BOOKCRAFT
SALT LAKE CITY, UTAH

Library of Congress Catalog Card Number: 97-78459

ISBN 1-57008-404-1

First Printing, 1998

Printed in the United States of America

Contents

Contents

Acknowledgments

Although this work is small in size we have received great help in learning about the lives of these women. For Maureen Ursenbach Beecher, Susan Easton Black, and James L. Kimball Jr., who have shared generously of their extensive knowledge of Nauvoo and its people; for the descendants of the women and the workers at the Daughters of the Utah Pioneers Museum who provided valuable help; for Janna Nielsen, editor, who is at once skillful, patient, and pleasant; for these and for Judy Nelson and Angie Hinckley, who read and reacted with insight, we are sincerely grateful.

— B. B. S. and S. W. T.

Introduction

THE WOMEN OF THE Church have long observed March 17, 1842, as the founding day of the Relief Society. Many are familiar with the story of Sarah Kimball and her seamstress wanting _Margaret Cook_ to make shirts for the men working on the Nauvoo Temple, and of the meeting with Joseph Smith over the Red Brick Store. But few know of the lives of the twenty women who were in that meeting the day Relief Society was begun. In these pages we acknowledge their compassion and their commitment and recognize the importance of their desire to unite their efforts in furthering the cause of Zion.

It was in the Nauvoo of 1842, as a continuing stream of converts arrived—many in need of help and a place to live—and work on the temple became a race against time, that a group of women opened their hearts and decided to form a charitable society. They took their idea to the Prophet

Joseph Smith and showed him a proposed constitution for the organization. Without hesitation he responded: "Tell the sisters their offering is accepted of the Lord, and He has something better for them than a written constitution."[1]   He then explained, "I have desired to organize the Sisters in the order of the Priesthood. I now have the key by which I can do it."[2]   He invited them to meet with him and some of the Brethren in the room over his store on the very next Thursday.

The women who gathered that day were of differing ages and circumstances. "The youngest were three teenagers, and the oldest, a woman in her fifties. Eleven of the women were married, two were widows, six were unmarried, and the marital status of one is unknown. . . . But they were and would continue to be one in anticipating that a women's organization formed under the direction of men called of God would be crucial to their . . . lives as Latter-day Saints."[3]

Joseph Smith directed the meeting, with John Taylor and Willard Richards of the Quorum of the Twelve assisting. He explained to the women the nature of the organization, taught them to use parliamentary procedures, and gave them an opportunity to choose officers. The women unanimously voted Emma Smith to be their president; she named Sarah Cleveland and Elizabeth Ann Whitney her counselors. The sisters chose Eliza R. Snow to be secretary, Phebe Wheeler her assistant, and Elvira Cowles treasurer. They decided upon a name and with that accomplished, Joseph Smith declared the society organized.

That the women chose Emma president would have no doubt pleased Joseph because she was his wife, but he might also have been pleased because in this action he could see the plan of the Lord unfolding. He told the women that the title "elect lady," given Emma years before by the Lord in a July 1830 revelation (see D&C 25), "meant to be elected to a certain work . . . and that the revelation was then fulfilled by Sister Emma's election to the Presidency of the Society."[4] He also read an epistle from the Apostle John, suggesting, as Eliza Snow later taught, that a similar organization for women existed in New Testament times (see 2 John 1).[5]

Joseph Smith attended the meetings of the sisters several more times during that first year to give instruction as preparation for their work. As he taught them he opened to their minds a vision of what the Lord had as a work for women. He gave them understanding of their places in the kingdom. He told them that in addition to looking after the wants of the poor and strengthening the community, they would have greater opportunities for learning, they would serve in an important relationship with the priesthood, and have the privilege, even the responsibility, to attend to their own salvation.

At the sixth meeting of the society, on April 28, 1842, the Prophet gave a lengthy and important discourse, and during this address he made the definitive assertion that "this Society is to get instruction thro' the order which God has established—thro' the medium of those appointed to lead—and I now turn the key to you in the name of God and this Society shall rejoice and knowledge and intelligence shall flow down from this time—this is the beginning of better days to this Society."[6]

And for that beginning we rejoice to this day. The Prophet emphasized that an organization for the women had always been integral to the Lord's plan when he said, "The Church was never perfectly organized until the women were thus organized."[7]

We remember with respect the women who attended the first meeting, who were there as the plan unfolded and as the key was turned. They, in a sense, represented each of us. In the following pages we give brief sketches taken from what is known of their lives as they went forth from that time, each empowered by the knowledge and experience gained in Relief Society.

These women not only represented all women of the Church in the founding meeting, they also typified Latter-day Saint women of their day. In even these small glimpses of their lives can be seen some of the faith, courage, and steadfast strength alluded to when it has been said that "their women were incredible."[8]

The women who met with Joseph and the other Brethren that March day in 1842, as they appeared in the minutes of the meeting and as they appear in the order of this book, are: "'Mrs. Emma Smith, Mrs. Sarah M. Cleveland, Phebe Ann Hawkes, Elizabeth Jones, Sophia Packard, Philindia Merrick [Myrick], Martha Knights [Knight], Desdemona Fulmer [Fullmer], Elizabeth Ann Whitney, Leonora Taylor, Bathsheba W. Smith, Phebe M. Wheeler, Elvira A. Coles [Cowles], Margaret A Cook, Athalia Robinson, Sarah M. Kimball, Eliza R. Snow, Sophia Robinson, Nancy Rigdon, and Sophia R. Marks.'"[9]

Emma Smith

As president of the Relief Society, Emma received a blessing under the hand of Elder John Taylor admonishing her to "be a pattern of virtue; and possess all the qualifications . . . to teach [the sisters] those principles requisite for their future usefulness."[10] The pattern of a close and caring relationship with her mother-in-law, Lucy Mack Smith, is one in which she excelled, taking her into her home and caring for her until Lucy's death. In obvious admiration of her daughter-in-law, Lucy declared, "I have never seen a woman in my life, who would endure every species of fatigue and hardship, from month to month, and from year to year, with that unflinching courage, zeal, and patience, which she has ever done."[11] Endurance, courage, zeal, patience—these could well be necessary attributes for future usefulness.

Emma accepted her new responsibility with

enthusiasm and a distinct confidence in what she believed Relief Society could become, saying, "We are going to do something extraordinary . . . we expect extraordinary occasions and pressing calls."[12] And as a beginning to their work she asked the members for help in finding employment for a sister whose husband had been killed at Haun's Mill, noting this sister's skill as a seamstress and as one who "is industrious—performing her work well."[13] Emma knew what it meant to search out the poor and needy. Her son Joseph Smith III recalled, "I remember that Mother filled her house with the sick who were brought to her from near and far, giving them shelter, treatment, and nursing care."[14]

She also knew that Relief Society did not deal only with caring for others, but helped women to become more Christlike, to enhance their homes, and to save souls. She urged that the sisters "divest themselves of every jealousy and evil feeling toward each other."[15] She instructed them in the female propriety and dignity of which she knew much; even years after her Relief Society experience, after the Saints had gone west, others said of her that she lived in a very genteel manner.[16] During the persecutions in Nauvoo, while the

Prophet was hunted and harassed and falsely charged, Emma led the sisters in circulating a petition among the women to plead for his protection from illegal suits. With hundreds of signatures of the women collected, she, along with Amanda Smith and Eliza R. Snow, traveled to Quincy and delivered the document personally to Governor Carlin.[17]

Then there came a period when Emma began having difficulties attending to her Relief Society duties. Most knew that she took exception to the practice of plural wives revealed to the Prophet. In this troubled time she kept mostly to her home. But her earlier effort to form a sisterhood among the women became of special value to her. Many of the other sisters, feeling her pain and remembering her years of sacrifice, prayed for her. In this way she realized a strength in Relief Society she could not have otherwise known.

The death of Joseph brought with it the necessity of separating what belonged to the family and what belonged to the Church—a delicate task in an operation where there had been so much of lending all one had to the success of the cause. Disagreements followed. In the end, Emma chose not to go west with the Saints.

Although she would never experience the fulfillment and peace most were to know as they built a home in the Mountain West, one does not soon (nor, indeed, ever) forget the years she labored giving heart and hand to sustain the Lord's work. Such as the time when, her husband in prison, she, "with two babies in her arms and two at her skirts, walked across Missouri, finally crossing the frozen Mississippi to refuge in Quincy, Illinois, carrying the manuscript of her husband's translation of the Bible hidden in pockets in her clothing."[18]

Emma *did* give the women a pattern of virtue that could be of future use to them. While she could not accept all of the doctrine and promises given to her husband, she filled an important, even sacred, role as the founding leader of Relief Society. And though she stayed behind, the legacy of her labors and her sacrifices came west with the Saints and remains a blessing to the Relief Society.

Sarah Cleveland

HEIR TO A FORTUNE, Sarah Cleveland had exceptional opportunities; she was well-educated and a woman of refinement and culture. After her first husband, a sea captain, died, she then married the manager of her estate. They had a son and a daughter. When the daughter was quite young, she and Sarah each had an identical dream on the same night. When Augusta, her daughter, came to Sarah to tell her of the unusual dream she had had, Sarah was surprised to realize that it was identical to the dream she had had on the same night.

The dreams were of a sacred nature and concerned a man dressed in a white robe who presented a rolled parchment with the invitation for them to "read." Written on the parchment in gold letters were the words, "Behold, I bring you glad tidings of great joy." This same thing was repeated twelve separate times. The twelfth time the man was encircled with a halo of light.[19]

Sarah respected the dreams, believing that she and her daughter would, in some way, receive "glad tidings of great joy." Later, when they went to hear the Mormon missionaries, the first to speak began by saying, "Behold I bring you glad tidings of great joy." Mrs. Cleveland investigated further and was convinced that what they taught was the true gospel. She was overjoyed. Her daughter shared her feelings, but her husband was of another faith and did not accept the message. Mrs. Cleveland and her daughter joined the Church, and as a result lost many of their former friends who believed that they were misguided.

When Emma Smith escaped from Missouri into Illinois, Sister Cleveland took Emma into her home in Quincy. The Clevelands suffered some financial reverses because of Sarah's affiliation with the Church, but they moved to Nauvoo, enjoying association with the Saints. Emma Smith chose Sarah to be her first counselor in the newly organized Relief Society.

When the Saints were going west Sarah wanted to go with them, but her husband said he would follow the Mormons no further, although he had been kind to the Church members. He even fenced a portion of his land where they could safely bury their dead during the persecution in Nauvoo. Sarah, who was very identified with the Church, would have gone in spite of his refusal, but Brigham Young enjoined her not to, for he believed Mr. Cleveland to be a good-hearted man. We have no record that her husband ever joined the Church, but Sarah remained true to her testimony and died in Plymouth, Hancock County, Illinois, in 1856, a faithful member of the Church.

Augusta, who married John Lyman Smith, did go west with her mother's blessing. She and her husband went to live in Idaho where they prospered and remained faithful to the truth she had long treasured.

Phebe Ann Hawkes

AND SHOULD WE DIE before our journey's through, happy day!"[20] These were familiar words sung along the trail. Two of the women who attended the first Relief Society meeting were among those who died on the journey west. As might have been typical in that day of few doctors and fewer hospitals, there were no clinical descriptions of the cause of death. "Died of exposure and hardship" was given as an adequate explanation and one most people seemed to understand.

Phebe Ann Baldwin Northrup lost one husband before marrying Joseph Bryant Hawkes. She lived in the community of Saints in Missouri, and after Joseph's wife died, leaving him with four motherless children, he and Phebe were married—she being thirty-four and he thirty-eight. One cannot help thinking of the blessing she must have been to the Hawkes's home, and also the joy that would have come into her life as well as the life of her husband. They had their first child, Amos, in March of 1838 in Far West; then in the fall of that same year, the Saints were driven from Missouri.

We can hope their years in Nauvoo afforded them some happy times. Association with the Relief Society sisters could surely have been such for Phebe Ann. She lost a baby just two months before the first meeting and could have found comfort and support among the sisters there. She would also have found strength in a focus on helping others, which can be healing to the heart and also bring joy in participation. Joseph's seven years of work on the temple placed him at the very core of creating some of the beauty for which the city was celebrated. But we know they suffered much heartache: from 1842 to 1847 two babies died as infants; a toddler died at two and a half years; one grown son of Joseph's died of consumption; and another at fourteen drowned in the Mississippi River.

In 1846 both Phebe and Joseph contracted a case of chills and fever from which neither ever fully recovered. Then in the fall of that year, after most of the Saints had gone, the Hawkes family and some others remaining had a serious conflict with persecutors and were driven across the river into the wilderness of Iowa. Although during these years they suffered many losses, they retained their faith in the gospel and their identity with the members of the Church.

In Iowa they struggled with sickness and poverty, got as far as Kanesville, and Phebe could go no further. The stress was too much for her. Broken in health, both of mind and body, Phebe died in 1850, leaving Joseph and two of the boys to go on to the West where they established a home and where her descendants yet honor her name.

Elizabeth Jones and Margaret Cook

❧

ELIZABETH HUGHES was married to William Jones. We know that she made the journey west, arriving in Salt Lake City in 1851.

Margaret A. Cook is another name listed on the roll of those who attended the first meeting. It has been supposed that she was *Miss Cook*, the seamstress with whom Sarah Kimball first discussed making shirts for the temple workers, but this is not certain.[21]

These sisters, known only by name, might be called the *everywoman* of Relief Society. Critical to the work, they often make a conspicuous contribution, as Miss Cook did. Their efforts nearly always make the difference between the success or failure of the work, but apart from their names, we know little of them or their history or their families. Perhaps in time the families of these two women at the first meeting will be found and can help in making the Relief Society's history more complete.

Sophia Packard

THE NAME OF SOPHIA Packard is always read where a list of the charter members of the Relief Society is given. She is also separately mentioned as the woman who seconded the nomination of Emma Smith for President. The Packards lived across the street from Emma and Joseph Smith in Nauvoo and were their close friends, so her action on that day gave expression to the warmth of their friendship. It also gave her a particular place in Relief Society history—the woman who seconded the nomination.

This fact in the life of Sophia Packard reminds us that our lives may also be known by what we "second." This single act on her part can prompt us to consider what we uphold in our lives, to see if what we "second" by our actions or words is what we believe.

When Noah and Sophia Packard were converted they did not hesitate to give whatever they could in support of what they believed. Noah went on missions, leaving Sophia to care for the family and farm; they sold their farm and contributed more than generously to the building of the Kirtland Temple and to the spreading of the gospel. The family actually lived for a time "principally on potatoes and salt,"[22] so substantial had been their contributions. When the body of the Saints were preparing to go west they gave again, this time to their son who had been called into the Mormon Battalion. He needed money to fulfill his responsibilities, so they gave him what they had saved for their trip west. They then worked and saved four more years until they could make the journey.

At length, they did come west, arriving in 1850 and settling in the town of Springville in Utah County. There they have a large posterity. Many to this day remember the heritage of dedication established long years ago in Ohio by Noah Packard, and many remember their maternal model Sophia who was quick to stand up for her conviction.

The organizational meeting of Relief Society provided an opportunity for Sophia to confirm her loyalty and friendship by seconding the nomination of Emma Smith. By its nature of providing service and promoting improvement, Relief Society gives opportunity for any woman who will seize upon it to make manifest her faith with her works, to second what she believes with what she does.

Philindia Myrick

WE KNOW LITTLE about Philindia Myrick (sometimes spelled Merrick). Tragically, she experienced the brutal murder of her husband, Levi, at the Haun's Mill massacre in Missouri. Philindia and her children escaped from the mob and made their way to Illinois, finally arriving in Nauvoo.

Emma Smith mentions Sister Myrick at the first Relief Society meeting as one who could benefit from the concern of the sisters. Pointing out where Philindia's husband died and commenting that she does fine needlework, Emma asked if there were any present or if the women knew of anyone who could employ Sister Myrick as a seamstress; this would enable Philindia to take care of her family.

Understandably, Philindia had struggled financially since the death of her husband, but she was managing because of her own efforts. In addition to taking responsibility for her family's needs,

Philindia was, even at that time, attending a meeting designed to help others. So although we haven't many historical records to tell us about this sister, some things about her are evident in the small bits of information we can piece together. Like many working single mothers Philindia may not have had much time for extra activities, but in Relief Society she could find associations to add joy to her life, knowledge to strengthen her faith, and (we learn from the minutes) help to meet her fiscal needs. In true compassion, Emma praised Philindia's abilities and recommended her for employment, not pity.

Before it was time to prepare for the westward trek Philindia had married a Brother Keeler who would help take her children to a new home in the mountain valleys. Here our story ends; we know only that she died on the way to the West. We can believe that her children were provided a loving home—the Saints were good at this. For Philindia, death meant a joyous reunion with a husband gone now eight years or more. Thus, we might conclude, "All is well! All is well!"

Martha Knight

LaDawn Palmer Toone relates stories told her by her grandmother Belnap about great-great-grandparents Martha and Vinson Knight, who opened the door of their farm home one evening to find Joseph Smith and Parley P. Pratt standing there. In exchange for a night's lodging, these brethren taught them the gospel nearly all of that night, and on the next day Vinson and Martha were baptized. In time, they sold their beautiful farm, went to Ohio, to Missouri, then to Nauvoo, Illinois. There are many scenes in these stories, including the terrible day that an open wagon brought the bodies of Joseph and Hyrum back to Nauvoo. But whatever else they include, always the ending was: "and Great-Grandma Knight was a charter member of the Relief Society." LaDawn concludes, "I wonder if she will be as proud of me as I am of her."[23]

This brief excerpt from a great-great-granddaughter's tribute is higher praise of Martha's life than could be accorded if we were to have a detailed description of her life told in her own words. What more would she want, or indeed would anyone want, than to know that one's life had mattered to her family, even to the third and fourth generation. Martha lived through the trials and persecutions that the Church as a whole suffered—from those in Kirtland to Johnston's Army's march through the Saints' new mountain home in the West. She had personal tragedies, including the deaths of her beloved husband and children, the falling from faith of one daughter, and the ordeals of old age and loneliness.

Through it all, her faith remained strong. Whatever the trials (and these included being run over by a heavy covered wagon and, at first, being presumed dead), she remained steadfast in her devotion to a life of service, leaving her family a legacy of love for the Lord and his work. We see evidence of this in her great-great-granddaughter's words and also in the remarkable experience of her descendants, who gathered on the plains of Nebraska to honor the grave of her thirteen-month-old grandson who died of cholera and was buried along the trail in his father's oak toolchest.

One hundred and fifty years after his death they came, scores of them, many travelling considerable distances, to mark the grave and dedicate the place that has become sacred not only by the memory of the little child but by the commitment of those who continue the trek in faith.[24]

Desdemona Fulmer

DESDEMONA FULMER might best be described as true: true to the faith that led her to Kirtland from her home in Pennsylvania, then to Missouri where she lived near Haun's Mill and ran to hide in the woods when warned of the mob. She experienced Nauvoo at a time when many were leaving the Church. Some derided her for continuing to follow a fallen prophet, but she remained true to her faith.

As a young girl she "praied," not unlike young Joseph Smith, to know which of the many sects she should join. She proved to be as faithful to her prayers as she was to the gospel when she received it, for she tells of praying "much in secret alone." When at last she received the answer of "a change of hart," she studied to know more by reading the Bible and learning about different churches. She writes, "Praid . . . alone to Lord."[25] Undoubtedly she had just neglected to add the article *the* before the word *Lord*, but reading it as it is there is a sense of personal address, as though she actually knew him. It is not hard to think of Desdemona feeling close to the Lord.

When she did hear the gospel preached by missionaries, Desdemona recognized the same spirit she had felt as she prayed. She accepted the teachings and baptism. Having once been convinced of the truthfulness of the Church and the reality of Joseph Smith's prophetic calling, she did not waver from that conviction, but remained among the faithful. The force of her conviction could be seen in her efforts to do good. When the women gathered to form a society to help others she was there to help. At the final exodus from Nauvoo she joined with the Saints who were going west.

She was a Saint. Just such people as she composed the body of the Church, and more particularly, the women of the Relief Society. Faithful, true, obedient, she handled trials as they came, but understood the ideal of a Zion that could be built through faith and toil. She lived her last years in Salt Lake City, admired by those who knew her. Contrary to what many feel—that one must do something great to be known for good—

she lived a great life built upon consistently doing the seemingly small but noble things, and always, as she said in the beginning, she prayed much.

Elizabeth Ann Whitney

IN ITS WELL-ORDERED way Relief Society may seem predictable and patterned, but for each sister it serves an individual need. Elizabeth Ann Whitney found—in her meetings with the women friends she enjoyed—a sisterhood and an expression for her deep religious feelings. Elizabeth knew from the first time she heard the missionaries' message that it was true, and she accepted baptism without hesitation. Elizabeth and Newel, her husband, found in the gospel the answer to their prayers; she lived it devotedly, and loved belonging to the Church. Once she wrote of what it meant to her: "A fresh revelation of the Spirit day by day . . . a most implicit faith in a divine power, in infinite truth emanating from God the Father, the fountain from which we must never depart . . . if we mean to conquer as individuals."[26]

Soon after their baptisms the Whitneys became acquainted with Emma and Joseph Smith.

The Smiths arrived in Kirtland needing a place to stay, and the Whitneys invited them into their home. This association began a close friendship and a lifelong trust. Although by following their faith Elizabeth and Newel were obliged to abandon their place in Kirtland, to lose their property and goods in Missouri, then to sacrifice for the building of the temple in Nauvoo, their belief in the Church and its Prophet never failed.

With a friendship spanning several years, it is not surprising that Emma chose Elizabeth to be her counselor in the newly organized Relief Society. When, as it turned out, times became difficult for Emma, and she could not always meet the pressing call of her office, she relied upon Elizabeth to carry on. Elizabeth did this willingly, for she loved Emma and had the deepest respect for the work. She remembered so well the teachings of the Prophet to the sisters and once wrote of Relief Society: "I realized in some degree its importance . . . . The Prophet foretold great things concerning the future of this organization, many of which I have lived to see fulfilled. . . . He prophesied, [things] that are great and glorious; and I rejoice in the contemplation of these things daily. . . . I trust the sisters who are now laboring in the interest of Relief Societies in Zion realize the importance attached to the work."[27]

Although the sisters found no opportunity to gather in meetings along the trail to the West, a stay in Winter Quarters allowed for such a time. Historian Marie Cornwall writes, "Women of faith met to enjoy what they repeatedly called 'spiritual feasts,'"[28] where they prayed, testified, and shared spiritual feelings. These gatherings fortified the women in the face of the sometimes heartbreaking scenes about them. Especially did they appeal to the spiritually sensitive Elizabeth Ann who, not only on the trek but all her remaining life, gave her effort to furthering the faith and the well-being of the women.

The success of Relief Society in its early years owes much to this saintly woman, known to all as Mother Whitney, who reared her eleven children and several more that would otherwise have been homeless; and yet also gave of her strength to help others. Her strength, which might have been called unusual, seemed to come from Relief Society itself, or more precisely, from her conviction that the work of women mattered to the Lord.

Leonora Cannon Taylor

LEONORA CANNON Taylor's family continues to be associated with the Church as it was in her generation, and it is replete with family histories. She had a good deal to do with her family's membership in the Church. This is the more interesting since she had immigrated to Canada and married there, while her family was still living in Britain on the Isle of Man.

Parley P. Pratt was told through prophesy: "Thou shalt go to Upper Canada, even to the City of Toronto, the capital, and there thou shalt find a people . . . [who] shall receive thee . . . many shall be brought to a knowledge of the truth."[29]

When he arrived in Toronto he tried in vain to find a place to preach. At the point of leaving, he stopped by the home of John and Leonora Taylor who had befriended him. He told Mr. Taylor of his intention, while at the same time Leonora, who wanted to hear his message, appealed to a friend saying, "He may be a man of God, I am sorry to have him depart."[30] The friend made arrangements for him to preach, and as a result the Taylors and others were converted. Some time later, John Taylor went to England on a mission and contacted Leonora's family, and thus through Leonora her brother George Cannon "turned his face toward the western world."[31] And so began the history of the Cannon family in the Church.

Leonora, who was described as having "unusual beauty,"[32] also had an uncommon sensitivity to the Spirit that enabled her to recognize Elder Pratt as a representative of the Lord when others did not. That same Spirit guided her during the long months her husband, who became a leader in the Church, served a mission to England; at the time he was severely wounded in Carthage Jail; and through the trials of camping at Winter Quarters while Elder Taylor was on a second mission. The trying conditions Leonora and the children experienced at that time are revealed in this short excerpt from her journal copied in the sketchy form in which it was found, that in itself tells us something of the conditions under which they struggled:

Mond 14th . . . Br Young calld about the Stray trunk, got S. Mitchell Babtised, Tud 15th returned the things I have got a dreadful headach George went to herd the Cattle got thrown from his horse one he had caught & put his whip acrost his mouth he got scared the lash came of[f] the handle of his whip and threw him, on his Arm & Split the Bone I took ime [him] to Doc Sprauge I bath it with wormwood and Whiskey I had a presentiment all morning something was going to hapen [to] him and spoke of it before he came home.[33]

John Taylor returned from his mission and took the family from Winter Quarters to the Salt Lake Valley where they once again established their home. He was sustained as the third President of the Church. In the same way Leonora recognized the Spirit giving direction in her life, we believe that she was able to hear with understanding the words of the Lord given to the women of Relief Society by Joseph Smith: "If you live up to these principles, how great and glorious will be your reward . . . ,"[34] for already in her life could be seen evidence of the promise.

Bathsheba Smith

HER YOUTHFUL AGE of nineteen made Bathsheba Smith the youngest of the married women attending the first Relief Society meeting on March 17, 1842. Although others had been married longer and were older, she may have had more experience than many in moving and getting settled into different houses. Five homes in one year! She and her husband, George A. Smith, the youngest member of the Quorum of the Twelve Apostles, tried a succession of them, looking for one with a chimney that didn't smoke and a roof that didn't leak. George finally built them a home to meet their needs.

When the persecutions required them to leave Nauvoo and their cherished home, Bathsheba used her domestic talents in equipping their covered wagon. Constructed with eight-inch projections on each side, it allowed for a bed to be placed across the end, leaving room for a table and chairs. These, along with the carpet on the floor and a hanging mirror, made it about as comfortable as a wagon could be.[35]

The teachings of the Prophet Joseph Smith in the early Relief Society meetings made a lasting impression on Bathsheba. She remembered and used them through the years. But in 1901, when she received the call to preside over the Relief Society, they became of paramount importance to her.

The year 1901 began more than a new century for Relief Society. It identified an era of changing trends for the women of the Church. They did not respond to the same programs in the same ways women had in the past. As general president, Bathsheba realized that "declining enrollment, and poor attendance of those enrolled, spoke undeniably of the need for innovation, yet she knew the society was grounded in revelation. She would need to look back to its origin and history for knowledge, example, vision, and achievements."[36]

Bathsheba's temperament served her well for giving innovative leadership. Her spiritual awareness and her ability to adapt were both critical components. She had faith in the Lord's concern for the women. A dream she had supported that faith: "In it she saw 'the Prophet Joseph watching over them.' The Prophet, she felt reassured, 'would look after Relief Society.'"[37]

As seen in her experience of trying to make a leaking log house into a fit abode and providing a covered wagon with the comforts of home, it is obvious that Bathsheba knew about adapting. Her believing heart was touched when the young Elder George A. Smith called at her lovely family home in the hills of Virginia. She believed the teachings, received baptism, and then had a confirmation by the Spirit of what she had done. She said, "The spirit of the Lord rested upon me, and I knew that he accepted of me as a member in his kingdom."[38] She knew by that same Spirit that the Lord had given Relief Society for all time and that as it fit the needs of the women in 1842, it would be relevant in 1901 and in every age.

Phebe Wheeler

THREE OF THE women at the first meeting did not come west because their husbands were not sympathetic to the move.

A widow at the time of the first meeting, Phebe Wheeler later married Oliver Olney. There is no information on record of their coming west. This may be because Oliver is known to have dropped away from active Church membership.[39]

Elvira Annie Cowles

"**I SOMEHOW HAVE** a great opinion of my Grandmother Elvira Annie Cowles, who died before I was born," wrote Congressman Milton H. Welling in 1938.[40] And well he might, for hers was a distinguished life made so by an unflagging faith that enabled her to consistently claim victory over near defeat.

The friendship and support of Relief Society sisters was important to her. Especially were they a strength when her father, who had been a stalwart member of the Nauvoo stake presidency, became a leader in a movement of spreading apostasy within the Church, causing a deep rift in their relationship. He would not accept the doctrine of plural marriage, and she, being sealed to the Prophet, would not give up the Church.

Elvira's two years serving as the first general treasurer of the Relief Society may well have been among her happiest. They provided her with a reservoir of spiritual strength from which she could draw during difficult times. She lived during those years at the Smith home, helping Emma. Later, Elvira married Jonathan Harriman Holmes for time. He also lived at the Smith home and served as bodyguard to Joseph. Brother Holmes' first wife had died earlier, leaving him with a young daughter, Sarah, in need of a mother.

The journey from this point became harder for this little family. The first child of Jonathan and Elvira died; then, as they were beginning on their trek west, Jonathan was called into the Mormon Battalion. This left his family to spend the coldest months at Winter Quarters without a father, in a log shelter, having neither door nor windows but only quilts hung over the openings to ward off the wind and chill. Elvira patched together what she could to outfit them for their move west in the spring. When the time came to leave, she and young Sarah—with their cow and ox team—started out. One day the cow lost a shoe and couldn't go another step. Elvira asked her captain what she should do. He told her to leave her wagon and little girl, walk back a few miles to the company just behind; there he thought she would find a blacksmith, and maybe he would be willing to come with her and help. She walked about ten miles, by herself, praying all the way that she would not come on to a wild animal or an unfriendly Indian. The blacksmith, being very understanding, did help her until she could be on her way again.[41]

Despite all of this, she made it to the Valley before her husband and taught school (with sego roots and wolf meat for pay) until he arrived. Jonathan came; they bought a home, and had three more children—daughters. All lived worthy, productive lives and provided Elvira and her husband a fine posterity. Had she lived longer she would have known "her children [to rise] up and call her blessed" (Proverbs 31:28) as Congressman Welling did in 1938.

Sarah Melissa Kimball

THE FIRST PAGE OF the Relief Society's history might well have been written in Sarah Kimball's parlor; for it was in her home in Nauvoo that talk of uniting the women led to the society. After considering the idea, Sarah invited some of the sisters to her home; they agreed upon an organization for relief of the poor. Coming together in this spirit gave the Prophet the key, as he said, to organize the women in the order of the priesthood.

In learning about the beginning of the Relief Society, we also learn something about Sarah Kimball. Along with her much-reputed keen mind and penchant for delving into doctrine (she was one of the few women who attended the School of the Prophets), we find that she had a deep concern for people, especially those in need. One example of this reminds us of the scriptural passage: "Lift up the hands which hang down"

(D&C 81:5). It occurred on a tragic June day in 1844. "The martyrs' mother could not be consoled; Sarah M. Kimball held her hand for a long time before the grieving woman spoke, 'How could they kill my boys!'"[42] Another time, as president of the Fifteenth Ward Relief Society, reporting to Brigham Young and Eliza R. Snow, Sarah indicated that the poor and unfortunate of her ward had been cared for "so far as we had the means and power to relieve and comfort them."[43] And in other records they were "provid[ing] food, clothing, and quilts for the poor," "paying tuition for poor children," and "mailing the *Woman's Exponent* to English sisters too poor to subscribe."[44]

As a Relief Society president, she turned her probing mind to searching out innovative possibilities for serving the sisters. Her Fifteenth Ward was the first to have a building of their own and a store for selling the products of the women's home industry. These were not the only "firsts." In fact, the Fifteenth Ward became a kind of flagship that led the way to what a ward Relief Society could accomplish.

Although it was Sarah's meeting that led to the formation of Relief Society, she was not chosen at the time to be an officer, or to have any special position, yet she continued to serve, to be a faithful member. This tells us another thing about Sarah Kimball's charitable nature that is nice to think on.

Women's rights and women's suffrage were favorite causes of hers and she made a great contribution to these efforts. But, although she had deep feelings, and was known as an outspoken person, she did not speak out on these issues until she knew the leaders of the Church approved of such a stand. Perhaps her clear thinking helped her to realize that by following direction she was able to serve the women and her "causes" well. Otherwise, she might have created a disturbance and accomplished little of benefit. She was sometimes called a woman who didn't mind saying what she thought, but knew and recognized and honored the authority of the priesthood.

Sarah M. Kimball, intellectual, humanitarian, activist, brought widely ranging interests and remarkable abilities to the Relief Society, and through them made an everlasting difference to the program. Her example underscores the fact that Relief Society is for every woman—God-given, for all his daughters.

Eliza R. Snow

THE RELIEF SOCIETY came west in several important ways; for one, in the carriage that brought the bags and boxes of Eliza Roxey Snow. Dubbed "Zion's Poetess" by Joseph Smith, Eliza, a schoolteacher, was known most extensively, even beyond the members of the Church, for her writing ability. She had quite naturally been chosen to keep the minutes of Relief Society from its beginning. And although the regular meetings were discontinued in 1844 due to the turmoil in Nauvoo, Eliza, as secretary, preserved the records and brought them safely with her to the West.

She must have realized the value of these pages that contained the account of the Prophet organizing the Relief Society and his instructions to the members on several occasions. They were irreplaceable. For more than one hundred and fifty years they have been used and are still prized as a continuing guide.

What Eliza may not have known was the extent to which her life would be identified with Relief Society. Although the formal meetings in Nauvoo were no longer held, the women did not stop their work of compassion and caring for the needy. Rather, the teachings they received, "to seek out and relieve the distressed," to be "ambitious to do good," to "have feelings of charity and benevolence," to "treat [their husbands] with mildness and affection,"[45] and more, were needed on their journey. It was as though Relief Society had been a preparation for their journey.

When they became located in their new cities and settlements, many of the women started holding meetings again, and Eliza Snow willingly helped them. In 1867, she was called by President Brigham Young to be general president of the Relief Society and to help establish organizations in every ward of the Church. This required her to go to settlements in remote places. She and her counselor, traveling by horse and buggy, were sometimes required to camp out overnight and were often obliged to repair buggy wheels and harnesses when breakdowns occurred. She did these things gladly because of her love of the Lord and her conviction that he held a blessing for every woman through the means of Relief Society.

For twenty-one years Eliza continued to guide the Relief Society, inspiring women to look well to the needs of their families and to aid any who were in want of assistance. She further counseled the women to then expand their world by enlarging their capabilities through study and to improve their circumstances through creative skills and industry. She taught that no woman should feel her life limited. "Don't you see," she urged, "that our sphere is increasing?"[46] Though she saw opportunities for women expanding, she always felt these to be enhanced and not curtailed by having the direction and blessing of the priesthood and the guidance of the light of the Spirit.

Eliza Snow's effectiveness in organizing the women lay largely in her conviction of its necessity. She demonstrated what she taught, that "without order we have no claim to the Spirit; we must have the spirit or we cannot remain organized."[47]

At her death the words from one of her poems, "no black for me . . . when I am dead," were observed, and for her funeral the sisters festooned the Assembly Hall with off-white muslin, green sprays, and white roses—a fitting memorial to an honored friend and mentor.

Athalia Robinson,
Sophia Robinson, and
Nancy Rigdon

TWO OF THE WOMEN who attended the first meeting of the Relief Society were the daughters of Sidney Rigdon: Nancy Rigdon and Athalia Rigdon Robinson. Another was Athalia's daughter, Sophia Robinson, who later married Lewis James. In Sidney Rigdon's falling out with the Church, these members of his family also drew themselves away from association with the Saints. Even at this distance in time one feels a sadness at their going. If there were such a thing as a door to this booklet, we would leave it ajar in the event that someone of their kindred should choose to turn back.

Sophia Marks

SOPHIA MARKS IS yet another who did not come west because her husband was not sympathetic to the move. William Marks was president of the Nauvoo Stake and a faithful leader in the Church until the point at which he had a doctrinal difference with Joseph Smith and chose to withdraw his membership.

Conclusion

IN READING OF THE lives of these sisters, remember that they were each one important to the Prophet and to the Lord. Joseph did not simply call together a set of officers, then give them the teachings and the key; they were all called. In each succeeding meeting others came and were added to the membership, until in little more than a year's time, the twenty had become 1,179 sisters, and was still growing.

Because their meetings continued in Nauvoo for only about two years, some might question if it had not been better for the Relief Society to have begun after the Saints were settled in the West. The answer is clear and emphatic. Relief Society had an essential place in the Restoration of all things. Historians Jill Mulvay Deer, Janath Russell Cannon, and Maureen Ursenbach Beecher have written: "No other authority than that of the Prophet could have brought Relief Society into being. He held the keys. . . . Only he was legally entitled to make the Relief Society an official part of the kingdom to bind it to the whole in heaven as on earth. Only through his authority, and by power of his priesthood, could he grant Relief Society the authority to act in all things within the scope of its commission."[48]

A major focus of all efforts in Nauvoo preceding the departure to the West centered on the Saints receiving their temple ordinances to fortify them for the trail. The teachings of Relief Society were an essential part of that effort, for they prepared the women for the temple. Likewise, the experiences in compassionate service, the knowledge of their role in the Lord's plan and of the Lord's consideration of them as women all gave them strength for the struggles to be faced in the journey ahead.

The same voice that gave Joseph direction and authority to organize the Relief Society resonates to each woman, as a member of the society then and now, giving her a part in the Restoration, an essential place in the kingdom of God, an assurance that she is known and needed by our Eternal Father and his Son Jesus Christ—strength to face the journey ahead.

Notes

1. "Story of the Organization of the Relief Society," *Relief Society Magazine* 6 (March 1919): 129.

2. Jill Mulvay Derr, Janath Russell Cannon, Maureen Ursenbach Beecher, *Women of Covenant: The Story of Relief Society* (Salt Lake City: Deseret Book Co., 1992), p. 41.

3. Ibid., p. 28. See also Maureen Ursenbach Beecher and James L. Kimball, Jr., "The First Relief Society," *Ensign* 9 (March 1979): 25–29.

4. In *History of the Church* 4:552–53.

5. See Derr, et. al., *Women of Covenant*, p. 28.

6. Ibid, p. 47.

7. "Story of the Organization of the Relief Society," p. 129.

8. Wallace Stegner, *The Gathering of Zion: the Story of the Mormon Trail* (Lincoln, Nebraska: University of Nebraska Press, 1964), p. 13.

9. Derr, et. al., *Women of Covenant*, pp. 27–28.

10. Ibid., p. 29.

11. Scot Facer Proctor and Maurine Jensen Proctor,

eds., *The Revised and Enhanced History of Joseph Smith By His Mother* (Salt Lake City: Bookcraft, 1996), p. 249.

12. Derr, et. al., *Women of Covenant*, p. 31.

13. Ibid., p. 3.

14. *Encyclopedia of Mormonism*, "Smith, Emma Hale."

15. Derr, et. al., *Women of Covenant*, p. 36.

16. Emma Smith remained an example of grace and charity throughout her life. "She continued to live her life with genteel qualities, meeting adversity and difficulty with grace and equanimity" (in *Encyclopedia of Mormonism*, "Smith, Emma Hale").

17. See Edward W. Tullidge, *The Women of Mormondom* (New York: Tullidge and Crandall, 1877), p. 296.

18. *Encyclopedia of Mormonism*, "Smith, Emma Hale."

19. Typescript from the files of Maureen Ursenbach Beecher.

20. "Come, Come Ye Saints," *Hymns*, no. 30.

21. "Story of the Organization of the Relief Society," p. 129.

22. Noah Packard, *A Synopsis of the Life and Travels of Noah Packard* (Salt Lake City: The Church of Jesus Christ of Latter-day Saints), p. 110.

23. From the personal files of LaDawn Palmer Toone.

24. See "Baby's Burial To Be Re-enacted," *Church News*, 26 April 1997; see also "Burial of Tiny Cholera Victim Remembered on Trail," *Church News*, 10 May 1997.

25. Derr, et. al., *Women of Covenant*, p. 5.

26. Elizabeth Ann Whitney, "A Leaf from an Auto-biography," *Woman's Exponent* 7 (1 August 1878): 33.

27. Ibid. (15 November 1878): 91.

28. Marie Cornwall Madsen, "A Legacy of Faith," in *A Heritage of Faith*, ed. Mary E. Stovall and Carol Cornwall Madsen (Salt Lake City: Deseret Book Co., 1988), p. 119.

29. B. H. Roberts, *The Life of John Taylor* (Salt Lake City: Bookcraft, 1963), p. 35.

30. Ibid., p. 36.

31. Janath R. Cannon, *Cannon Family Historical Treasury*, p. 19.

32. Ibid., p. 32.

33. Carol Cornwall Madsen, *Journey to Zion, Voices from the Mormon Trail* (Salt Lake City: Deseret Book Co., 1997), p. 199.

34. In *History of the Church* 4:605.

35. Tullidge, *The Women of Mormondom*, pp. 342–43.

36. Derr, et. al., *Women of Covenant*, p. 152.

37. Ibid., p. 151.

38. Tullidge, *The Women of Mormondom*, p. 150.

39. See *Journal History*, 19 October 1843.

40. Milton H. Welling in *The Ancestors and Descendants of Job Welling, Utah Pioneer from England 9 Jan 1832–7 March 1886*, comp. Emma Taylor Moon and Marlene Moon Bowen (Bountiful, Utah: Carr Printing Co., 1982), p. 19.

41. Phebe Louisa Holmes Welling in ibid., p. 24.

42. Richard Neitzel Holzapfel and Jeni Broberg Holzapfel, *Women of Nauvoo* (Salt Lake City: Bookcraft, 1992), p. 130.

43. Jill Mulvay Derr, *Sarah M. Kimball* (Salt Lake City: Utah State Historical Society, 1976), p. 9.

44. Ibid., p. 11.

45. *History of Relief Society, 1842–1966* (Salt Lake City: The Relief Society General Board Association, 1967), pp. 19, 21; see also *History of the Church* 4:605–6.

46. Derr, et. al., *Women of Covenant*, p. 36.

47. Quoted in Derr, et. al., *Women of Covenant*, p. 63.

48. Derr, et. al., *Women of Covenant*, p. 48.